Enhanced Eerie Elegance

More Halloween Party Ideas & Recipes
with a
Touch of Spooky Style

by
Britta Peterson

Britta Blvd Publishing

Enhanced Eerie Elegance is an original publication of Britta Blvd Publishing.

Britta Blvd Publishing
2532 Rose Way
Santa Clara, California 95051 USA
publishing@brittablvd.com

First edition: July 2011

Printed in the U.S.A.

Enormous thanks to...

My editing and development crew, whether early on or in the final crunch:
Natasha, Tracia, Ruth, Jules, and my mom Diane.

All my fellow Halloween fans from all over the globe.
It is always so much fun to hear from you, and some have even become good friends!

My Creepy Cuisine Contest Winners who were so kind to give their permission to
include their creations: Dave & Wendy, Tracey, Ruth, Tracia, Lyle & Glen

All my party guests, friends & family over the years for being my captive audience,
and inspiring me to show them new ideas every year!

I hope you enjoy Enhanced Eerie Elegance!

Table of Contents

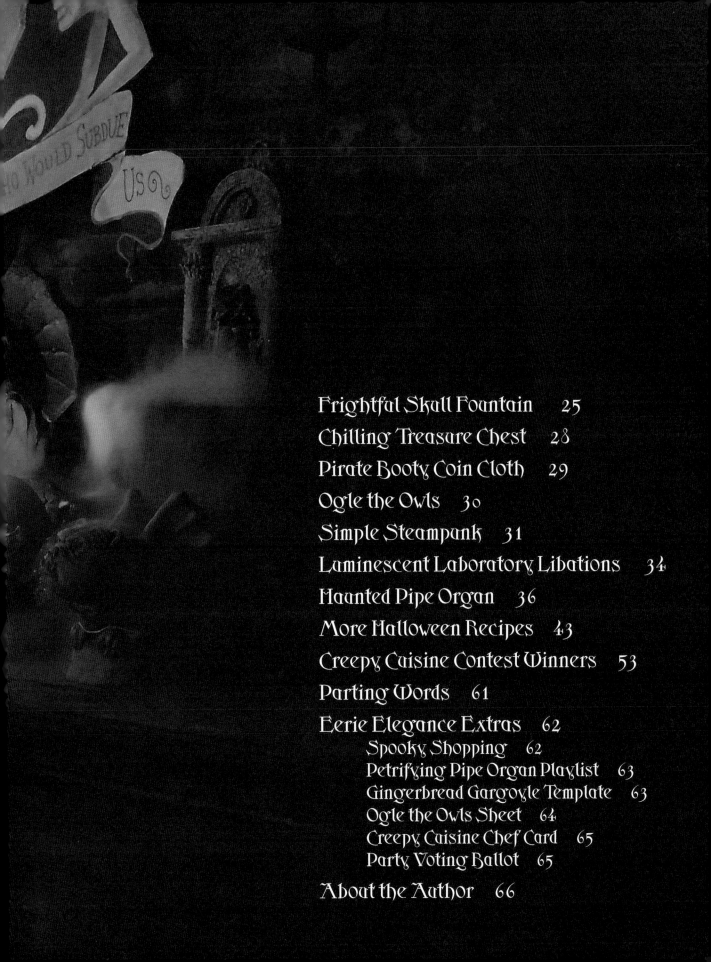

Introduction by
Britta, Webmistress of the Dark

Welcome to Enhanced Eerie Elegance! This book builds on ideas and concepts presented in the first Eerie Elegance book, with new techniques from simple to advanced for enhancing your eerily elegant parties. I always want something new each year for my guests to enjoy, and I enjoy making the new ideas myself. After about 15 years of hosting, I have many ideas to make the world smile with a touch of spooky style.

Many of these enhancements have developed from my moves over the years from apartments to houses giving me room to expand my decor, including more storage space for the off-season, but you can adapt the ideas to your own living space. Remember you can always pick and choose the ideas you like best to start simply, then elaborate over time, which is exactly what I have done over the years.

You will find basic party hosting advice and sample to-do lists in the first book, so let's jump right in with some new projects and recipes!

Faux Flames

eal candles give authentically ancient atmosphere and lovely lighting, but they not only can be dangerous with open flames around children or draping costumes, but can also make messes of melted wax, and can give off too much unwanted heat. There are various ways of creating Faux Flames with no mess, no heat, and only slightly less light than real candles.

Lighting technology has come a long way the past few years, so now realistic flickering LED battery tealights are available quite inexpensively almost everywhere. The easiest way to use them is inside candleholders that never show the flame or candle directly, then no one will ever know you are using an LED instead of a real flame. For other candleholders or other sizes, especially ones with spikes to hold the candles stable, you will need to get more creative.

Battery Tealight Sleeves

To support battery tealights over spikes, you need a sleeve, but one that will support the weight of the tealight on the bottom edges. I used craft foam sheets that were already black for my black candles. Cut the foam to the desired height, tall enough for the tealight to sit on top of the spike, with just enough overlap for a seam. Holding the foam

tightly enough to stay in place on the tealight, hot-glue the seam the entire length of the sleeve, and that is your first wax drip. Keep using hot glue to make more wax drips of varying lengths until you like the result. Remove the tealight from inside and spray paint the candle

sleeve your desired color. Turn on the tealight, slide it back into the sleeve and set over the candleholder spike. You can make these sleeves for any size tealight, votive or pillar LED candles. Since these are created from foam and hot glue, there is no risk of melting in summer storage.

Pillar Candle Sleeves

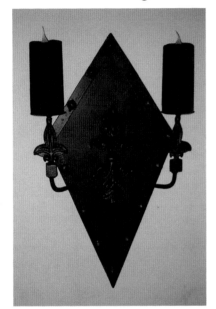

If you are lucky enough to find larger pillar LED candles, you still may need to accommodate spikes before you can use them where you like. I found these on Christmas clearance extremely cheaply, and since the tops were already a nice melted shape, I didn't want to create a full sleeve. I used the same black craft foam and cut it tall enough to clear the spike

but exactly the circumference of the existing plastic pillar so there was no overlap. I carefully hot-glued the foam so it would be flush with the pillar side and

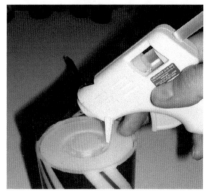

glued the seam. Since the plastic pillar is very light, the foam cylinder base supports it just fine. I masked the bulb with tape, then spray painted the entire pillar black. In place on my spiked wall sconces they look very realistic and no wax mess on couches or the wall anymore, especially black wax that stains!

Wax Tealight Sleeves

You might have pillar or larger real wax candles that you like, perhaps already melted into interesting shapes but the wicks are buried, or burning them further will make too much mess or burn them away completely. You can drill out the center of the wax candle so you can place an LED tealight inside, keeping your candle the same forever. Get a paddle drill bit large enough for a battery tealight to sit with a little clearance around it. A 1.5 inch paddle bit, also called spade drill bit, was just right for my tealights, but check your sizes before you do all the work. Burn the candles down for artistic wax edging, snuff the flames,

then when they are cool but still soft, drill out a hole deep enough to hide the battery tealight. Contain the wax shreds by drilling inside a box, otherwise they will fly everywhere. You'll drill out the wick so it won't be a functioning real flame candle anymore, but this way you can save the colors and shapes you like from year to year and avoid melted wax messes. With these you can still stick the wax housings on candle spikes for stability.

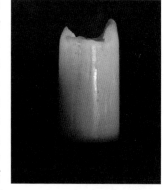

You can either grasp the flame bulb to remove the tealight, or dump the whole candle upside-down if the tealight sits too deep. This technique works best with 3" pillars or wider, otherwise you risk cracking the wax when drilling too deeply. These look the most authentic because they are wax just like real candles, but you run the risk of them melting if your summer storage gets too hot.

Battery Taper Candle Sleeves

You've probably guessed by now that I have quite a stash of LED tealights to use all over my house, however LED taper candles are still too expensive to be practical. You can still find inexpensive battery taper candles with incandescent bulbs, but they are always white tapers. I do not want white candles for Halloween, so I make colored sleeves for my battery candles. The extra bonus of this method is that you can make multiple colors of sleeves and use them on the same set of battery candles for different holidays.

You need something very thin for taper candle sleeves otherwise there will be too much girth to sit in your taper candle holders. I have found that thin acetate for scrapbooking pages is cheap and thin but sturdy enough around the battery candles. Cut a piece of acetate to wrap around the candle, use hot glue to anchor into a tube shape, keeping enough slack to easily slide the battery candle out. Now that you have one wax drip along the seam, keep adding hot glue wax drips artistically around the entire candle sleeve until you have the effect you like. Let dry, then remove the sleeve from the battery candle and slide onto a scrap stick or tube, then spray paint whatever color you like. Satin finish or matte gives a more authentic wax look rather than gloss paint. Once the paint is dry, slide the sleeve back onto your battery candle and display.

You can use the clear bulbs as they come with the candles, and arranged around your décor they are quite effective, even though they do not flicker. However to enhance this even further, dip the clear incandescent bulbs into clear silicone caulk and hang to dry, leaving a tapered flame tip. The caulk will dry opaque enough not to see the bulb filament, but translucent enough the steady light will show through. I have looked everywhere, but I still cannot find flicker incandescent flicker bulbs that work on battery circuits, even though I have plenty that work in plugin fixtures. I think they use alternating current to create the flicker effect, so they cannot work on batteries. If you ever find any, please let me know!

Old Stone Walls

For several years I covered my interior walls entirely with flagstone gossamer to simulate block castle walls, as described in the first Eerie Elegance book. This is a fabulous effect with impressive results that transforms your entire space, but it not only is time-intensive, but you must be exact in cutting around windows, doors, and other obstacles, tape enough to hold up the full wall length of gossamer, plus attach a lengthwise seam because the patterned gossamer is only sold in 5-foot widths.

In my travels I am always keeping my eyes open for inspiration for any projects, especially when touring old castles, so I had noticed many old buildings had plastered over stone block or brick walls, and over the centuries plaster had worn away in sections, revealing the original block structure, like the old British estate attic shown here. I decided I could decorate my walls this way by cutting the flagstone gossamer with random curved edges to simulate the plaster wearing away, leaving the normal wall color as the plaster. Not only does this still look impressive,

but it is much easier, since you no longer need to worry about working around windows and doors or climbing all the way to the ceiling edge, plus you can use 5-foot wide chunks without adding a seam. You must tape around the edges enough so that the curves stay put instead of fluttering or folding from gravity, but that is still less tape on your walls than taping the entire perimeter of your room. Originally I used foam mounting tape which sticks great and removes from most painted walls okay, but it is bright white and will show through the gossamer, which on white walls is fine. After I painted my walls tan with an aged plaster technique, I found clear double-sided removable poster tape that is perfect. It never removes any paint or does any damage to the walls, but since it is not quite as sticky as the foam mounting tape, you need more pieces of tape to anchor the gossamer. Keep track of where the tape is when you're removing the gossamer for storage, otherwise it's so clear that you might still find tape on your walls months later!

Ghostly Greenery

When I think of Ghostly Greenery, I immediately think of Dusty Miller, also known as silver ragwort, or *Jacobea maritima*. It is bright silvery gray with soft velvety hairs covering the foliage and rounded lacy edges instead of traditional-looking leaves. I have one that I bought as a small plant that has lasted over 4 years in my garden, now grown into a large bush because I keep trimming the blooms and pruning it back so it doesn't get too leggy. It is an excellent renewable source of Halloween floral arrangements for me!

The most basic idea is to arrange your Ghostly Greenery as a cut arrangement in a vase or other watertight container and place anywhere, like a buffet table. Lately I have seen stalks of chili peppers shaped like miniature pumpkins sold as cut flowers in the fall season, and those are adorable paired

with Dusty Miller cuttings, Purple Hopseed Bush, and some Coleus if the plant is large enough for cuttings.

However, the majority of spooky plants I find are not appropriate for cuttings at time of purchase, so I arrange them together in pots and urns. I have large stone urns that fit a 5-gallon pot, so I have been known to squeeze the smaller plastic growing pots just as purchased into the 5-gallon pot for the party, then take them out afterwards so the separate plants can be planted in the correct place in my yard or turned into potted plant displays so they can survive for next year. My urn arrangements are often supplemented with tall pruned stalks from my large bushes of Dusty Miller and Purple Hopseed Bush.

Follow the Fog

You can easily use Dusty Miller by itself for a striking look, add some other plants for color or texture variety, and you can even add bubbling eerie fog to enhance the ghostly effect! The low-tech way to create ghostly fog is to use dry ice. To conserve how much dry ice you need, you can use smaller watertight containers that fit between your outer container and inner plant container, then put the water and dry ice in those containers. Glass or ceramic can be dangerous if they break from the extreme cold of the dry ice, so plastic is

better. Always wear gloves when handling dry ice, and never let it touch any exposed skin. My first attempt was to cut a plastic plant saucer to nest between the pot and the urn, and that worked well since the saucer was shallow enough that all the fog spilled over the edge. You will need to refill the dry ice to keep the fog effect going, and warm water works best for the most active rolling fog.

If you have an electricity source near your arrangement, you can use water mister devices, often sold as "mist makers." These have been sold for several years at specialty stores, and they only need a couple inches of normal water for the mister to generate fog. Some misters come with built-in color-changing lights that can add to the spooky effect. You will need to refill the water over time because the mister is evaporating the water to make the fog. Since the

misters require a certain depth of water and do not work submerged in too deep or too shallow a container, this works better in window boxes or arrangements where you can hide the mister container between pots or vases. The misters give a more subtle spooky misty effect, not the rolling quantities of fog that dry ice provides.

For either dry ice or misters, make sure the top of the fog container is positioned at the rim of the outer container, otherwise your fog will just float down inside the container instead of spilling over the outer edge.

Favorite Flora

I started using just Dusty Miller for my arrangements in black urns that showed the fog, then I started seeing more possible combinations with interesting plants while strolling my local gardening stores, especially dark purples that almost look black. For a short-term arrangement for a party, it doesn't matter if the plants need the same light or water requirements as each other, but if you're trying to keep your investment alive over time to use again, you might want to keep them in separate pots to split them up later. Often a quart or gallon plant can be split and repotted as smaller sections, which makes your budget go farther.

I have kept track of many of the plants I have enjoyed using in various combinations. These are mostly shades of purple and black, but I sometimes add splashes of orange along with the purple, black & silver for a more festive Halloween look, depending on my mood and what I happen to find that shopping trip. Keeping these plants alive in your yard year-round will depend on your climate, but everyone should be able to use them short-term for parties, and possibly even as indoor houseplants.

There are several varieties of *Heuchera* that are mottled purple like decaying ghostly flesh.

New Zealand flax (*Phormium tenax*) is a dark purple spiky grass, perfect for vertical height and textural variety.

Many varieties of *Coleus* are variegated with various purple shades or streaked with bloody red centers.

Sedum hybrid 'Purple Emperor' is a good medium height plant with plain purple spiky leaves radiating from central stalks.

Purple Hopseed Bush (*Dodonaea Viscosa 'Purpurea'*) grows to a large bush of all reddish purple oval leaves on tall branching stalks, great to prune to add vertical height in arrangements.

Black Mondo Grass (*Ophiopogon planiscapus 'Nigrescens'*) is a short mounding thick-leafed grass that starts deep purple and turns black, perfect for Halloween! It drapes nicely as a short fringe around the edge of a pot.

French lavender has silver foliage and purple blooms, nice and tall for height in arrangements, but they need well-drained soil and plenty of sunshine when planted in the ground.

Curly Rush, also known as Corkscrew Rush (*Juncus effusus spiralis*) is a grass that grows in spooky spirals.

If you're lucky, you might be able to find the tropical houseplant Purple Passion Velvet Plant (*Gynura sarmentosa*), which has deep purple hairs covering the leaves just like plush velvet, but I have only found it once!

Devilish Decorations

Mix and match projects from this chapter or use them as inspiration for your own designs to create your own spooky party atmosphere.

Glowing Crystal Ball

This effect is so easy no one believes it! All you need is a color-changing LED battery light, which can be found now even at discount stores for $5 or less. Add a frosted globe lightbulb cover as the crystal ball, set over the light on a candle stand, and you have a glowing crystal ball. If you have a clear globe instead of frosted, you can add iridescent fabric artfully scrunched into the globe to diffuse and hide the light source. Different stands will give different looks to your crystal ball, so look around thrift stores or even your own house until you find your favorite look.

Spiderweb Lantern

My front porch light is excellent for security the rest of the year, but it is much too bright for Halloween, and my porch is too dark without any light at all. I used the same fabric from my spiderweb lace curtains to make a cover for my porch light. You can use this same technique for any lantern-style light fixture, whether portable, on a lightpost or mounted on a wall.

Take a sheet of scrap paper or newspaper that is large enough to wrap around your lantern to use as a pattern. Trace around the edges of the glass at the top and bottom of the lantern, as well as where the paper overlaps for the seam in back. Remove the paper, lay out flat, and trim where you traced. Wrap around the lantern again to adjust the fit if necessary. Once your paper template fits the lantern, use the template to cut your fabric to the same shape. Use fabric of medium opacity, since too sheer the light will shine too much, and too opaque no light will shine through. If your fabric will fray, cut around the template enough to sew a hem, or use no-fray hem glue found in fabric stores. Overlap the fabric in back enough to add a strip of hook & loop tape so the lantern cover will stay on but be easily removable.

Spiders Spiders Everywhere

What is spookier than an infestation of spiders everywhere you turn? This is an extremely simple idea that does take time to set up, but is very effective once complete. Just about everywhere sells bags of plastic spiders during Halloween season, and you can buy them year-round online. The more spiders you have, the more effective the final display, so get at least a bag of 100 or more. Place the spiders crawling around anything and everything, picture frames, in a trail along decorative shelves, in plants or floral arrangements, or hanging on chandeliers. The more unexpected the better, so when your guests finally notice, they really jump!

Tree Trunk Trash

One of the great challenges of party planners is how to hide trash cans in a clever way. Most attractive trash cans are too small for practical use for large parties or only fit in certain decor, so it ends up being just another ugly big plastic can marring the special environment you so carefully created for your guests.

One of my solutions was to build a façade for my ugly big plastic can that looked like a tree trunk. I saved brown grocery bags and craft packing paper until I had quite a pile. I covered the plastic can and my work surface with large plastic trash bags so the can

could be removed for cleaning, then I started building papier mâché around the can using the sturdy brown paper, rolling some into logs to give a more interesting trunk shape. After many layers of papier-mâché, I had a good semblance of a tree trunk even for color and texture. However I decided I wanted more crackly bark and more structure, so I continued by covering the entire trunk with drywall spackle, adding grooves with a putty knife for the bark texture. After the entire outside was dry and set, I removed the plastic can so I could finish the top edge. Since the spackle was white, I painted several layers of various colors of brown to pick up the bark texture and give it depth. When finally finished, it definitely looked more interesting than the plain plastic can!

Skeleton Hand Wreath

My original Halloween wreath was dark woven grapevine with black silk roses, black and purple ribbon, and small skulls I made from polymer clay, long before any stores had started selling wreaths specifically for Halloween. Over the years stores started selling Halloween wreaths very similar to mine, so I had to come up with something new and different. Luckily I found a whole stash of small plastic skeleton hands at a discount

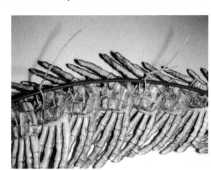

store, sold in packages of 10 for $1! I bought a bunch then wired them together in pairs of hands through the holes conveniently already in the palms. Just stacking them flush was too dense and didn't show off the fact they were hands, so I spread them out by adding a bend in the wire between each pair of hands.

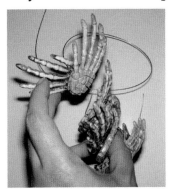

They overlapped nicely and created a good curve, but the wire that fit through the holes was not heavy enough to keep a circle when hung on the door. I snipped the extra rings away from a heavy wire floral wreath form so it would hide behind the hands, wired the hands to the wreath wire, and added the skull knocker to the top as a focal point. Now this wreath functions as a knocker as well as looking spooky!

Terrifying Trophies

Since I have been giving prizes at my parties for years, I have had many ideas of prize medals or trophies to give to winners. I had ideas of skeleton trophies on my list for years but ran out of time each year to make them. When I saw them for sale cheaper than I could make them, I started thinking of other ways I could make my trophies terrifying.

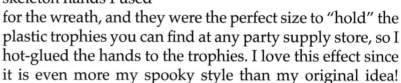
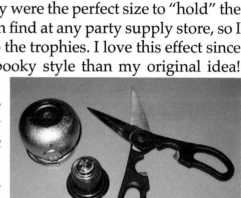

I had leftovers of the cheap small plastic skeleton hands I used for the wreath, and they were the perfect size to "hold" the plastic trophies you can find at any party supply store, so I hot-glued the hands to the trophies. I love this effect since it is even more my spooky style than my original idea!

For the Creepy Cuisine trophies, I had party favor black plastic cauldrons already, so I snapped off the trophy from the base, cut a hole in the bottom of the cauldron so it snugly fit on the base post without glue, and separately spray-painted the cauldrons gold before adding them to the trophy bases.

To finish your trophies, either handwrite on the base using a gold paint pen, or use label paper and your computer to print out your prize categories, trim to size then stick on the trophy base. If you don't give away all your trophies, you can always remove the label and print a new one for the next year. If you can find gold inkjet label paper then even better!

Gravestone Garnishes

If you have become an expert at carving your own gravestones from the first Eerie Elegance book, you probably want to garnish your gravestones to make them even more authentic. If you have toured as many cemeteries as I have, you will notice that the oldest gravestones often develop moss and become overgrown with ivy or other vines. It's a bit much to have your entire graveyard overgrown the same way, so choose the gravestones you'd like to embellish, leaving some plain as well. Here are some real gravestones from England to help inspire you.

Get some green, brown and black acrylic paint, a paint plate or palette and a brush to blend colors together, a paper towel or sponge, and a bunch of floral ivy and other vines. You might find U-shaped floral staples when you buy the ivy, but it is easy enough to make your own out

of plain wire. Just use wire cutters for a small piece, then bend into a U shape. They will be pointy enough to stick into the foam just fine. Don't make them too long so they stick out the back of your gravestones!

For the moss method, mix green, brown and black paint together so it almost looks too black. Test by sponging onto your gravestone and keep mixing the colors until you have the effect you like. Plain green is too bright for the gravestones I have seen in reality, and it often darkens to almost completely black.

To decorate with fabric or plastic vines, arrange them like they would be growing from the base of the gravestone, and anchor them with the wire staples. I found more bunches for sale than long strands of floral ivy, but that still worked since I used the bunch at the base so it looked like the vine was rooted there, tucking in the large stem along the back of the base and hiding it with a strand. Drape the longer strands climbing up the gravestone, anchoring with wire staples along the way, and leave some strands reaching out along the ground at the base, like it would grow naturally.

You can mix and match the moss and vine techniques any way you think looks best for each gravestone. Some can stay just mossy, some can have only vines, and some can have both. Arrange them in your graveyard according to what would grow where, and where visual interest is best. For instance, I positioned many of the vine-covered gravestones away from my living plants so the vines would be noticed. Tuck some other gravestones among your real plants, too, and now you have a very realistic graveyard!

Carved Stone Walls

My first foray into carving foam was to make my own gravestones, as described in the first Eerie Elegance book. After making so many gravestones, I had plenty of practice cutting the foam insulation sheets to shape and using my wood burning tool with dimmer switch for the carving, so I was eager for larger projects!

Of course you need the space for this, but since I had moved to a house, I wanted to change my patio entry to an archway door with stone walls, and the foam carving technique was perfect. You must work out your design in advance, since the foam only comes in 4-foot by 8-foot sheets, so you will have seams to make a larger wall. Plan for your carved block effect to use those seams to their greatest advantage.

For the gray house, a plywood-backed sheet was required to hinge the attached door, but the other foam sheet was directly bolted to the stucco wall behind it. Since the stucco was already gray, the faux stone walls were painted to match and blend with the interior décor. I used the flagstone gossamer pattern as my guide to carve the block effect.

Anchoring the foam to existing walls can be a challenge. When I tried to anchor them to the stucco at the gray house, I tried using large washers and long bolts into the stucco wall. Then I covered the bolt head and washer with a foam cap that nested into the carved block pattern. That works but any wind will still tear the foam away from the bolts even with large washers, so fair warning! I have been lucky at my current house to have a screened patio so I can wedge the foam walls between the floor and ceiling so that they stay in place. For that to work, you must measure accurately when cutting your walls, especially if you have a slanted roofline like I do.

You might be able to design something freestanding like my shed chapel. I designed a bell tower that rested on the shed roof but slipped tightly over the top seam of the two front wall pieces, so the bell tower and tree branches held the walls in place. I also cut the corners of the tower so they would interlock without glue enabling the pieces to store flat.

Once you have your design planned, cut the foam to the proper size for your design, including doorways if needed, and any anchor covers or other details. Lay out your walls with matching seams together, preferably outside or somewhere with good ventilation, since the melting foam fumes are not good to breathe in closed spaces. Lightly sketch your carved design onto the foam while you heat up the wood burning tool, using a dimmer switch to control the heat level and a long extension cord to give you plenty of room to maneuver. Once the woodburning tool is hot enough, start carving your design into the foam. I found for the large blocks, the largest woodburning tip worked well, then I kept the tool moving but left it nice and hot so it melted the foam very quickly, jiggling as I went along the line to make the jagged stone edges. Turn the heat down for finer lines to draw cracks or other intricate designs. If you want to add more depth, you can cut and glue more foam pieces to the surface, like over the archway. I originally did that out of necessity because the arch had broken at the top so it needed reinforcing.

After all the carving and gluing is done, paint your basecoat with water-based paint so that no white is showing. I used matching gray to blend with the gray house, but when I moved to the tan house, I was able to reuse some foam wall pieces by trimming them to the angled roofline and repainting them to match the new house.

Once your basecoat is completely dry, use spray paint and a garden hose to age the walls. Matte black spray paint works with gray basecoat, but dark brown aging looks more natural on the tan basecoat. Prop the walls at a slight angle over grass or some other surface that will not be harmed by water or paint overspray, then age the walls by alternating gently spraying water and paint, mimicking centuries of dirt and rain as it dribbles down the wall. You might need several attempts before you get the best results, since what looks good up close for gravestone aging isn't as effective at a distance for larger walls. I did age the walls in the first photos, but it was hard to see, so I redid them more dramatically when I added the gargoyle columns and had to paint them to match.

Even if you store these carved foam walls carefully, you may have some breakage or deterioration over the years. By adding reinforcements like the thicker archway design, or columns to hide seams that start disintegrating, and touching up paint to cover the white where anything has broken, you can make them last quite a few years. If they have finally become unusable for their original purpose, and you don't have another use like carving into new gravestones, don't worry, since they can become ruins in another display!

My shed chapel walls had a hard life stored on the shed roof since I had no other space for them. Not only did they blow around the neighborhood once in a winter storm breaking off a chunk, but rats decided the foam was tasty enough to chew holes all the way through in spots, plus the tree above dropped rotting fruit and leaves that eroded the surface including the paint, so they were quite a mess after 5 years. All the better to be ruins, my dears! I painted and aged the back sides to match the fronts, added some dark green paint with a sponge to simulate moss, and bought a bunch of cheap floral ivy and other vines to anchor with wire to the overgrown ruins, using the Gravestone Garnishes techniques described earlier. Tied to the front tree so they wouldn't blow away, the wall ruins made a great backdrop for Pirate Corner!

Fiendish Fortress Doors

Pointed Gothic archway doors are a feature in castles and manor houses, but not very common in modern homes, so adding a Fiendish Fortress Door or two to your décor transforms it immediately.

Since most modern door openings are rectangular, you need to make a door frame to match the shape of the door. The most difficult issue is making the archway around the door stable enough for a hinged arch door to work properly. My first attempt was 2-inch thick insulation foam but braced with wood strips where the hinges attached, using the foam cutout as the door but covered in fake wood paneling that I painted to look more realistic. This almost lasted through the party but only by propping it open, not letting guests open and close the door themselves. You could do the same by propping the door open instead of having a functional door that opens and closes, then you wouldn't even need wood reinforcements.

For the next year I tried reinforcing the entire archway with thick plywood, using construction adhesive to glue the foam to the plywood arch, but that was very heavy, and the foam door still had issues where the hinges screwed in the door. By the next Halloween, I had moved to my own home, with a screened patio structure where I wanted my archway door. This was perfect since I could fold back the screen door and use the screen door frame to anchor my arch door, but the foam door was too thick. I had already started remodeling my house in the summer, including removing some fake wood paneling from inside, so I cut matching arch doors from the paneling to sandwich together as a thinner door, adding chunks of 2x4s to reinforce the hinges. The foam archway is now purely a façade that rests in front of the door that is hinged to the metal screen structure.

Regardless of how you anchor the doorway, you need to make an arch door. Fake wood paneling works well but it is too thin to use a single panel, so sandwiching two panels back to back works better and creates a nice thin door. You will need to add thickness at the hinges or they won't have enough body for the screws to hold the door. I did this by adding scraps of 2x4s just for the hinges and anchored them through both panels.

Vintage arch doors usually have iron strap hinges, often in very elaborate designs. Since that's one of my favorite parts of Gothic doors, of course I designed my own strap hinges and cut them from thin MDF or paneling with my jigsaw and painted them black to look like iron. To be sure they match, cut the first one, then trace around it for the second one. You can purchase real iron strap hinges online, but they are

$100 or more each! I first made my curly hinges for the foam door and since they were only screwed in, I was able to remove them and reuse them with very short screws for the paneling door at the next house. To make the 2x4s blend in on the back side of the door, I cut simpler strap hinges that met the edge of the 2x4, then painted the 2x4 black to match. I added a cheap black powder coat gate handle on each side to use the door. For both the hinges and the handles, you need to be careful you aren't trying to screw at exactly the same spot on each side of the door since it is so thin!

When I moved in, my shed had no doors at all, so I asked my father to help me build some. We could have made simple doors, but since the shed has such a prominent place for Halloween and I like the look all year, we built slightly arched fortress doors instead. This outside house paneling was stamped with a woodgrain texture but primed a flat beige, and it was sturdier than the interior fake wood paneling, but we still reinforced it with planks on the back side and inside the metal door frame, especially where the hinges anchored, since these doors would be in use year-round for the shed. I found $8 black powder coat gate hinges that were decorative enough for my budget, but I did splurge $16 online for the weathered iron slider bolt closure. After my father helped me build everything so the doors worked, I removed the hinges and doors, sanded the hinges so they wouldn't be so glossy, and painted the doors with several coats of various brown washes of acrylic paint.

This is the same painting technique I used on the foam door fake wood paneling to give it more realism. Water down some brown acrylic paint, and brush it lengthwise "along the grain" into

the texture, letting it pool in the grooves if you have them. Let that coat dry completely, then see how much darker you need to go before you have the look you want. It shouldn't take very long for each layer to dry because the paint is so thin. I kept adding a small bit of black to my brown paint little by little until I had enough layers that I liked the wood effect. The more thin layers you paint, the more depth you have so it looks like real woodgrain. I still have people completely shocked when they realize they are not real solid wood doors!

Gargoyle Columns

Ever since I found cardboard tube concrete forms for sale in my home improvement center, I have wanted to make them into columns, but I never had the space until I bought my own house. I was planning on making my own gargoyles, but I found a pair of resin gargoyles cheaper than I could make my own, and I liked the idea of guard dog gargoyles at my castle entrance.

I had scrap thick foam insulation from previous projects, and two apple boxes were the perfect square size and shape for the column bases. The largest foam squares fit over the apple boxes with a groove in the foam the width of the cardboard edge. This locks the foam onto the box for stability but comes apart for storage. The next foam square for each column has a circle cut entirely through so it tightly fits onto the cardboard tube. This foam square is glued to the largest foam square, so the cardboard tube stands inside the circle. For the top, slightly smaller squares were cut

in the same way, with the lower square having a circle cutout for the tube, then the top square mostly solid, with just a little impression cut to match the circle base of the gargoyles. I used 3" dowels and drilled matching holes in the bottom of the resin gargoyles and the top foam, so the dowel helps the gargoyle stay in place. These columns stack together and are fairly stable with weights like ceramic tile or bricks in the apple boxes, but they are not glued so they easily come apart for storage. I use them in a sheltered location, away from rain and too much breeze.

Once the columns were built, I painted everything including the resin gargoyles with the basecoat tan color to match the stone walls, so they would look like the columns were carved whole from the same local stone. When the basecoat was dry, I used the now-familiar aging technique of

21

water hose and spray paint to dribble decades of dirt. Dark brown spray paint works best for the tan basecoat, and I was careful not to get the cardboard tubes or boxes too wet from the hose. With these Gargoyle Columns flanking the Fiendish Fortress Door, it makes quite a foreboding castle entrance!

Spooky Spellbooks

For many years I was looking for old books or cheap hardback books to make into old sorcery books for Halloween decorations, but I was never as successful as I'd hoped, so I decided to make my own. I saved boxes in various book sizes like cereal boxes, cracker boxes, and cake mix boxes, along with flat corrugated cardboard from shipping boxes. Disguising cardboard is second-nature to me, so the bindings were no problem, but I was expecting the most work to be getting the page edges to look like paper. Lucky me, I spotted "string cloth" contact paper that looks perfect!

Select one of the boxes and lay on flat corrugated cardboard. Trace around the front, spine and back like wrapping a present, leaving room for the cover to be slightly larger the page box so there is an overhang like hardbound books. Cut out the cardboard and score at the edges of the spine where it will wrap around the box. If you want a rounded spine, carefully score the spine lengthwise from the inside and gently bend into a curve that will stick out slightly away from the box. Using plain craft paper, wrap the cardboard like a gift, so all the raw cut cardboard edges are covered with paper. This is your "fabric" book cover. Tape is sufficient to anchor the paper cover on the inside, and you do not need to cover the entire inside flaps front and back with paper since those will be glued to the box.

Choose the base color of your book cover, and use spray paint to cover all the craft paper. You will need two painting sessions, one for each side after the other side is dry. Metal primer makes a great brown fabric texture, and you can use any colors you like. If you are making several books, it is easiest to spray paint all the matching colors at the same time. Use sticky notes or something to help you remember which cover goes with which box!

While the paint is drying, decorate your inside page boxes. If you cannot find string cloth pattern self-adhesive contact paper, cover the exposed edges of the box with normal paper and create a paper edge effect by dry-brushing with paint or drawing lines. Using the string cloth contact paper is much easier, believe me!

After all the paint is dry and the inside boxes look like pages, hot-glue the covers to the boxes, centering the cover overlap around the box. Now you have a very lightweight fake book! All you need is a title on the front and spine. You can download free fonts online and print out your book titles on scratch paper, then use carbon or graphite paper to trace the printouts onto your book cover surface and spine. Once you have the lettering traced onto the book, go over the lettering in silver or gold paint pen. If you want to age your books, you can use brown, green & black paint to sponge moldy spots over any place on the book you think looks appropriate.

Storage is easy because they are so lightweight and fit well in cardboard boxes. You can display your books on a shelf with just the spines showing, stacked horizontally to give height to other items or food displays, or standing behind other props to show off the clever titles and decorative front covers of your Spooky Spellbooks.

Dastardly Dangles

I used disposable plastic cups for my parties for years, but then I found a price for the popular skeleton hand goblets that I couldn't refuse, so I bought 2 dozen! But how can guests tell their drinks apart? Dastardly Dangles of course! Craft stores have more and more Halloween tree mini ornaments for sale in cheap sets, and there is always fun inexpensive Halloween jewelry too.

Add some wire and beads and charms from a local bead store, and you can make your own goblet charms.

I use the same metal wire I've had for years but you can use fancier wire if you like. The easiest charm shape can clip around a goblet stem or hang over the side of a cup or glass, so they are very versatile. Cut a length of wire about 3 to 4 inches long. Bend a loop in one end, curve into a U shape, then start adding your beads, charms and mini ornaments in the patterns you like. Adding different colors of beads to the same charm will be a different enough combination. Once your

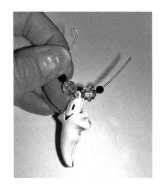

design is in place on the wire, bend a matching loop at the other end of the wire to keep them in place. Bend the U shape into more of a C shape that just fits around the goblet stem without falling off, but still easily removable. Keep making as many as you need for your party!

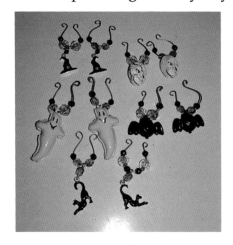

Frightful Skull Fountain

Punch fountains have been around for years, and inexpensive models have been for sale recently. When I found a plastic skull funnel for sale one year, it inspired me to make one of my plastic cauldrons into a punch fountain, with blood-red punch bubbling up and spilling over the edge of the skull.

First I decided which plastic cauldron would be sacrificed to the cause, and cut the skull funnel neck to a good height, not too tall above the edge of the cauldron with room to attach the fountain pump at the bottom. The skull funnel neck was thin plastic that was bendable on purpose, so to stand up straight it needed some support. I found a plastic pipe that fit inside the neck just perfectly, then cut the pipe to the exact length so it just peeked out the inside of the base of the skull. I had also acquired a skeleton hand candleholder that looked perfect resting on the edge of the cauldron.

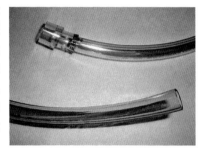

I knew from previous fountain pump experience you need a tight seal around the edge of the pump or the liquid leaks out instead of making the distance through the fountain. I bought plastic tubing at the hardware store that fit my pump and also fit inside the plastic neck support tube, so I had to nest them together at the pump end for a tight seal. I left the tube longer since I had hoped to make an ice brain to sit inside the skull. (I did test the ice brain, but the moving punch melted the ice so quickly, it wasn't worth the effort.)

Adding the pump into the cauldron was a little trickier. I drilled a hole large enough for the fat grounded plug to fit, so the electrical cord didn't have to drape over the top edge of the cauldron. I aimed the hole so the cord would come out next to the flat cauldron base, not wobble on the cord, nor too high so it would be difficult to hide. This cauldron had a small hole in the center bottom, so I filled both the hole around the electrical cord and the bottom center hole with silicone caulk. At the same time, I glued the pump to the bottom center since the suction cup feet did not want to stick to the plastic cauldron surface. I taped everything in place and let the silicone caulk cure. The trickiest part is getting it watertight! No matter how well you thought you sealed the

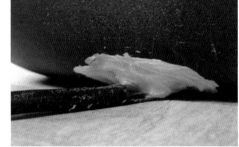

first time, you will always need to test with water to see where it leaks, let it dry completely, then seal again with more silicone. Even once you get it watertight, if it is stored in heat, by the next year you might have developed a new leak. Test with water each year before your party so you don't end up with a sticky red punch mess all over your floor!

Once the skull is full of liquid, it is much heavier so will tilt from being top-heavy, spilling everything all over. Just supporting with wire from the back edge of the cauldron wasn't enough support, so I designed a cauldron handle that "happened" to be propped up just under the skull, then used thick coat hanger wire to bind the handle around the

neck. The wire is anchored to the cauldron by cutting holes in the cauldron's plastic rolled edge just barely large enough to tightly fit the wire, then bending the wire inside the edge to stay in place. The handle plus the wire from the back gives three-way support, which is good enough to support the skull from falling either direction, even when full of bubbling punch. I

used the same thick coat hanger wire to anchor the hand to the cauldron edge so it can be removed for cleaning. Since I used heavy electrical wire that did not match the cauldron, I removed the hand, masked off the skull and inside of the cauldron including

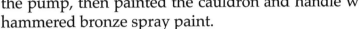

the pump, then painted the cauldron and handle with a metallic hammered bronze spray paint.

After fully testing everything with plain water and happy with how it worked, I added a little splash of bleach to the water and let everything run for about a half hour, sanitizing the entire path and the cauldron, just as restaurants sanitize their food preparation surfaces. Even though I had purchased a brand-new fountain pump and used new plastic tubing, I wanted to be sure it was clean for punch. I dumped the bleach water, then ran plain water again through the fountain for another half hour to rinse away

any residual bleach. Definitely clean the fountain this same way after each use before storing it, or you could have a sticky mess before next year!

Now you are ready for punch! You must be careful about the liquids with the pump. You cannot use anything with pulp like pineapple juice, for fear of clogging the pump mechanism, and if you use more than 25% of carbonation, the pump will not work anymore. Since I wanted this to be non-alcoholic punch and this was a medium cauldron, I used two gallons of deep red cran-raspberry juice with only one 2 liter bottle of lemon lime soda for fizz. Of course I added dry ice, using the spice ball technique for the large cauldron so no one could accidentally scoop any dry ice chunks into their cups. I also added a couple small chunks to the skull since no one was scooping punch from the skull, and the dry ice is heavy enough that even with the fountain motion, the chunks do not escape over the side of the skull. It takes awhile to fill a cup from the trickles streaming over the skull, so I

had the bone ladle available for spooning punch from the cauldron too. With the skeleton hand goblets around it and the fog bubbling it looked fantastic in the corner of my Halloween party!

Chilling Treasure Chest

My friends know to offer me any interesting trash they have, since I might make something out of it! This time it was a foam ice chest that came with some frozen steaks, and it was more

of a box shape than the usual cheap foam ice chests. I had been brainstorming more decorative ways to keep drinks cold for theme parties, so I thought of building a treasure chest around the foam.

I had taken down an old slat fence by my shed, and I had kept the wood in case of projects. There were enough the same size so I used them as the treasure chest slats. My handy brother helped me design and measure around the foam chest, plus donated the

scrap plywood for the sides. He also let me use his chop saw and pin-nailer, which made the project so much easier! We cut all the slats to the right size and sanded what we could, but since the wood was so old and weathered, plus there were

different colors of wood, I knew I would be painting it instead of staining. Two slats braced across the bottom for support, but the sides were just pin-nailed to the thick plywood, including

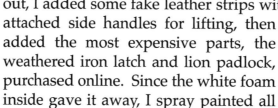

plywood half-circles for the sides of the lid. Standard heavy hinges on the outside attached the curved lid. After I painted it brown inside and out, I added some fake leather strips with nail brads for a trunk look,

attached side handles for lifting, then added the most expensive parts, the weathered iron latch and lion padlock, purchased online. Since the white foam inside gave it away, I spray painted all the foam black, and the foam sits in the base on one long vinyl strip to work as handles to lift out the foam.

Not only does this look great for ice keeping bottles cold, but you can also load it with booty for a pirate display when not using as an ice chest!

Pirate Booty Coin Cloth

I had already used the Chilling Treasure Chest as an ice chest, and I had always wanted to do a display like Pirates of the Caribbean, but that meant I needed a lot of pirate booty and bling. You can buy plastic gold coins almost anywhere, but to fill an entire chest or set out a big pile is still not cheap. All you need is to cover the

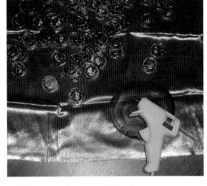

top visible layer, but I didn't want to glue coins to the actual chest. Why not glue the coins to gold lame fabric that will drape over anything underneath?

I had gold lamé already in my fabric stash but you can buy some new for reasonable prices at the fabric store, and you'll only need a yard or less. The sparkly gold is so any space seen between coins still looks like more of the same gold. Lamé is very thin, so make sure it is on a surface that will not be damaged by any glue seeping through. I used scrap cardboard to protect my surface. I bought 144 plastic coins in bulk at a discount party

store, then started with the hot glue gun. I measured the rectangle I needed for inside my chest, and aimed for some overlap to the sides so when it was draped it would still have plenty of coin area. A perfectly flat surface of coins will not look realistic since they would sit in piles. Overlap the coins a little when gluing them to the lamé so they look random but still have enough surface contact between the coin, glue and fabric. If you overlap them too much, the coin cloth will not drape as well. Test for the draping effect by putting something underneath the cloth, and add coins to any gaps you don't like. If you need a freestanding pile of booty, glue coins all the way to the edges of the fabric. I tucked the edges into the chest for this cloth. It will take awhile to glue all the coins, but when it is finished, you have a magic pile of coins you can use anywhere. Fill the chest or pile with scraps of anything like recycling that will give you the random shape you need, cover with the coin cloth, and you have a shiny pile of booty ready for pirates!

Ogle the Owls

This is a decoration idea that is also a game! By now I have quite a collection of owls in many shapes, sizes and styles, so I count them all, arrange them around the party inside and outside, then provide a quiz sheet for my guests to write down where they saw

each owl. Whoever finds the most is the Outstanding Owl Ogler. Not only does this help guests meet new people by giving them a common goal that is not a timed event, but it also "forces" your guests to pay close attention to all your decorations so they will fully appreciate them. An example quiz sheet is provided in the Enhanced Eerie Elegance Extras section. You can use any collection of similar items that are recognizable as the same category, perhaps black cats or gargoyles could work as well as owls. Be careful to count all your collection, since some might be hiding where you've missed them yourself!

Simple Steampunk

I have loved what I have called the "vintage science fiction" look for decades, inspired by authors Jules Verne and H.G. Wells, but recently that style has acquired the name "steampunk" with thousands of people online creating wonderful items, costumes, and even hosting conventions. My original concept for the screened patio of my new house was to change it for Halloween into a manor library, with bookshelves lining the walls, but it took a few years to find the right way to execute my plan within budget, even adding real hand-me-down bookcases, a dark wood bar and my grandmother's china cabinet to the patio year-round. When I finally found the perfect bookcase wallpaper murals online, I decided it was time to change my Mad Scientist Laboratory from the modern white lab coat style to the Library Laboratory, add my own costume as intrepid explorer and experimenter Miss Hermione G. Wells, and go all out with steampunk, but as inexpensively and simply as possible!

What is Steampunk?

Steampunk is Victorian styling with techno elements like ray guns, computers with typewriter keys, zeppelin airship aviators with brass goggles, and lots of wood and brass with rivets. Gold spray paint is cheap, as is woodgrain contact paper, so I was able to change many of my existing props to steampunk style, adding some thriftstore and trash finds as well.

Sometimes you'll get lucky and find items you do not even need to alter. Fancy-looking but cheap resin toothbrush holders can work as test tube holders, and the tall gilded clock, book box and tray were from a discount home store.

For my costume I made a utility belt where I could hang my ray gun, vintage keys, and other tools any explorer would need. I found a pirate play set for $1 at a discount store, but I changed the black and silver to wood and brass by spraying the entire

gun gold, then when dry going over the gold with a dry brush technique using brown acrylic paint until it looked enough like wood. I also needed brass goggles, so I masked off the rubber seals and clear lenses from a $1 set of swim goggles, spray-painted them gold, and changed the strap to an old brown fake leather belt with some black elastic sewn to the ends.

Gold paint works great, but adding rivets really finishes the steampunk look on even the simplest items. I bought many craft store possibilities like gold plastic beads of various sizes plus some self-adhesive scrapbooking brads, and tried what looked best for each, using clear glue to hold the beads in place.

Even an old black candleholder has now become a steampunk beaker warmer.

Some of my favorite items were home remodeling scraps, like the extra vent tubing from my kitchen remodel, the vent cap and valve handle from my water heater replacement, and some copper pipe from both projects. Painted gold they look completely in place in the new Library Laboratory, especially with a nefarious light from inside the vent. This is exactly why I never throw interesting things away.

The oscilloscope is another favorite. It was broken when I acquired it, but it has been a fantastic prop in the modern scientist lab unaltered for years. I wanted to keep using it in the Library Laboratory, but I needed to steampunk it. A few minutes of measuring wood contact paper, some gold tape around the strap edges, with a wash of gold acrylic paint over the metal handle and face, and voilà, it fits right in!

However, I think the most dramatic Simple Steampunk transformation was the $1 lime green plastic straw dispenser. Again just some gold spray paint and a few rivets, add some black straws inside, and I like the result so much it is used all year on my bar!

Luminescent Laboratory Libations

Ever since I turned my lab display into a mix your own experiment activity, I have been looking for ways to make edible liquids glow safely. There are references online that spinach juice or milk will glow under ultraviolet light, but I have tested them and they haven't worked for me. The only ones that are reliable are tonic water with quinine that glows blue, even diet tonic as long as it has real quinine, and vitamin B-12 glows green. Some sports drinks have B-12 in them, but not enough to glow, so I have crushed B-12 vitamin pills into dust and added one pill to 2 quarts of

water. That glows a nice green, but it tastes absolutely horrible! Mixing tonic and B-12 together gives a beautiful glowing aqua teal color as shown here, but since I don't like tonic either, I can't even drink it. A little black vodka on top gives some nice shading.

I have given up on the edible iridescence and moved onward to using colored lights under the bottles and in bowls of ice cubes. This works quite well, but requires some crafting and some investment in the lights. For the lighted bases you can use any colored tealights, even color-changing lights, but if you want to use the lights in the same

container as ice cubes, invest in submersible floral lights shown here that are safe to use completely submerged in water. I have found them online for about $3 each plus shipping, and they are great. They are slightly smaller than normal tealight size, they twist on and off instead of a switch, and the batteries last a long time. I tried them first with purple, and they give off enough ultraviolet spectrum to make the fluorescent items glow, so then I bought an assortment of colors, including a few color-changing lights. The color-changing lights are really fun, but I like having others stay one color so there is variety in the laboratory.

To make the bases you need containers that are opaque so you don't give away your light source, and they need to be large and flat enough to safely support your bottles, but not so large that light escapes around the bottle. You might find some candleholders that will work, an old light fixture base, maybe a small decorative box, or even a scrap of large plastic pipe. Once

you have found the bases, you need something to diffuse the light source. I went through my stash of plastic containers and found some translucent lids that were perfect. I sanded some to-go container lids to make them opaque enough and trimmed them to size. I also tried some crackle sheets from the home improvement store that are sold as large panels for ceiling lights. Be careful cutting the crackle sheets since they are

brittle and tend to shatter. The lids need to stay removable since you need to put the lights inside. If your lid doesn't nest inside the edge of the base, make sure it has a lip over the base edge so it doesn't slip off when party guests are using the bottles.

Turn on the colored lights, place them in the bases, cover with the lids, set in place with bottles, beakers and flasks, and now you have Luminescent Laboratory Libations!

Haunted Pipe Organ

I absolutely love pipe organs even though I can only play them at a basic proficiency. When I can finally build my own small castle, I intend on having a real pipe organ in the grand hallway! Until then, I've always wanted a pipe organ as a Halloween decoration. There was no way to build or store one at my apartment, so I drew a tromp l'oeil organ with chalk on black paper, and that worked well for years since I could roll up the paper and store it in a closet. You can even have an unseen ghostly pipe organ by playing my favorite spooky suggestions for pipe organ music included in the Extras section at the back of this book.

When I moved to a duplex with more space, I tried to enhance the paper version with foam to make it a quasi-3D effect, but I didn't really like it, so a real pipe organ has been on my Halloween decoration list for a while. My plan was to build a plywood box to surround my various electronic keyboards so the pipe organ decoration would be playable, but as it happened, I got lucky!

A few years ago a house around the corner from me was doing a major remodel, and as I walked by I saw an old 1960s electric organ on the street. I asked what was happening with it, and the owner was giving it away. It had no wheels, so I needed help moving it. I asked her workers nicely to drive it 6 houses around the corner for me. Perhaps my short skirt and sleeveless shirt helped convince them, since they kindly obliged. It made some ugly noises, so I knew the speakers still worked. It didn't work properly, but I loved how all the broken keys pressed down looks like a ghost is playing it. With some lifting help, I put caster wheels on it so I could move it around by myself, then I was able to work on it over time, and store it out of the way the rest of the year. The first year I was able to get the pipe organ presentable just in time for Halloween. I saved my elaborate grand vision for embellishments over later years!

Haunted Pipe Organ

For this project, you will need

electric organ, working or not, plain style is fine
scrap pipe in various widths, all 2 feet or longer, plastic is good for lighter weight
primer spray paint (optional)
silver or gold spray paint
scrap plywood
scrap wood for pipe box surround
scrap studs for bracing support

for decorative embellishments:
cheap decorative shelf (optional)
scrap foam sheets from packing material, gravestone leftovers, etc
black paint
gold paint

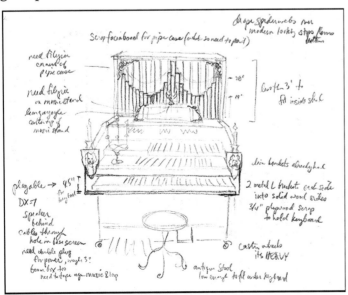

Many thriftstores have electric organs, but they usually still work so are priced higher than I personally would want to pay for a Halloween decoration. Some neighborhoods have cleanup weeks with street pickups where homeowners can set out large items, or Freecycle or Craigslist might have people trying to get rid of a big item like an organ. If you still can't find an organ to use, you can use my original plan of creating a plywood box around working keyboards. The trickiest parts to make realistic from scratch are the keyboards of a real pipe organ, so using real keyboards makes the project much easier.

The first year my pipe organ lived in the "graveyard chapel" otherwise known as my garden shed. I hung black gossamer curtains from wire to hide my garden shelving and the organ just had enough room in the center. With only one spotlight overhead and battery candles, I wasn't as worried about the external decoration until later years, so I concentrated on the keyboards and pipes that I knew would show at night.

I acquired free scrap PVC pipe in various sizes from various sources over time, including scraps from my old sprinkler system. Even though I have taken pictures of pipe organs around the world in my travels that are gorgeous and elaborate, I was restricted by my space, so this is more of a chamber pipe organ, with a simple rectangular pipe box. This not only makes it easier to build, but also makes it easier to move around, since the pipe box is a separate piece that sits on top of the organ and can be lifted off easily.

I had scraps of 1x6-inch fascia board that were perfect to create the pipe box, so I set out the pipes I had and arranged them to look realistic. Real pipe organ pipes are displayed for aesthetics more than function since you never see all the pipes you actually hear, but they usually are arranged in order of width. I put my largest pipes on the sides and center and arranged the rest between. I had a lot of the same width, but they still work since I also created a simple symmetrical curve to show pipes at a range of lengths for different pitches. Since the pipes were various lengths to begin with, it was a bit tricky figuring out which could be behind or in front. As you can see, some of my front pipes covered back pipes that were too short for the height of the box.

After I laid out the pipe plan, I cut the pipes to length with my reciprocating saw, and sanded the ends. The top back pipes were hot-glued temporarily for positioning, then I screwed them from the back into a scrap piece of plywood which then was screwed to the top back of the pipe box. I used the only two long pipes for vertical support at the ends since they fit tightly into the box. Since the larger pipes were a mix of gray, black and white smaller ones, I used white spray primer before the silver, and I sprayed the back pipe rank separately before putting them into the box. I didn't have another piece of plywood the right size to do the same brace across the back of the front rank of smaller pipes, so I hot-glued those to a piece of cardboard just for positioning, caulked them to the bottom of the outer pipe box from the back, then screwed

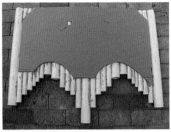

them to each other and to the back rank of pipes wherever I could for stabilization. After all that was dry, I masked off the pipe box surround and sprayed all the pipes silver. Since my fascia boards were primed white, I regret that I did not paint them black before I assembled the box and added the pipes, so please learn from my mistake!

Now it actually looked like a pipe organ, but it didn't sound like one. The easiest plan would be to have a soundtrack nearby playing pipe organ music on a loop, easily accomplished by any media player with accompanying speakers, however I wanted my guests to be able to sit at the pipe organ to play. Thankfully I still

have my 1980's classic Yamaha DX-7 keyboard with full-size keys and pipe organ patches! Since the electric organ already had 2 keyboards, I added a shelf underneath to hold the playable keyboard, and drilled a hole at knee-level through the speaker cover for the electrical cords to pass through so they would be hidden. Since they keyboard is quite heavy, I used scrap ¾-inch plywood with two solid metal L brackets on each side for support. So far, the brackets and silver spray paint were the only purchased items for this project!

I cut some curved brackets out of wood scraps to help hide the metal ones, and a pair of cheap lion curtain brackets had been waiting for a project, so flanked the playable keyboard. I added a couple little carved wood embellishments and a lion gargoyle to tie in with the lion brackets. A wash of black paint over everything helped blend it all together, especially in the dark lighting, and

my antique piano stool was perfect in front. With my iPod playing my pipe organ playlist on repeat over a speaker and the playable keyboard hooked up to its tiny amp hidden in the corner of the shed, the Haunted Pipe Organ was definitely a hit its first Halloween!

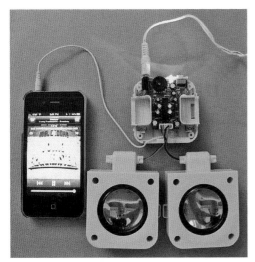

Enhancing the Haunted Pipe Organ

Now that the basic pipe organ was a success, I had plans to make it even better. Not only did I want to make the decoration more elaborate, but I wanted to make it more efficient than all the accessory audio electronica required the first year.

I knew the built-in speakers from the original electric organ still worked, but not the key mechanisms, and I wasn't sure how safe the old power supply would be over time. The power supply issue was easily solved since I could bypass it completely by using a grounded extension cord connected to a power strip, and plug everything into the power strip at the back of the keyboard shelf for easier access from the front. As for the speakers, I traced the wiring and identified what I thought were the audio wires, so I cut them away from the organ with as much slack as possible. I knew from prior experience that speakers do not need separate power supplies. I had a cheap $5 iPod portable speaker unit from a discount store, so I cut its little speakers away, then attached the central unit speaker wiring to the organ speaker wiring. I had traced the wires correctly, since it worked, complete with on/off switch and volume control! That central unit used a power block that plugged into the power strip, and plugging in my iPod with a stereo mini cable worked great!

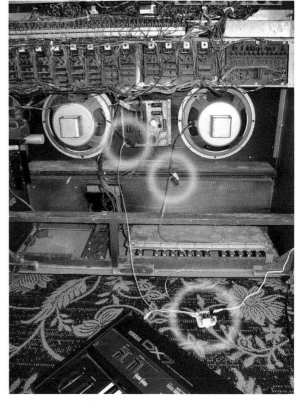

Now how to add the playable keyboard into the new audio setup? I got a y-cable so both the iPod and keyboard could connect to the new central unit, but even though that was easier to connect everything from the front side without crawling around back, one must be unplugged for the other to be heard, so no playing along with the pipe organ soundtrack anymore. What I needed was a small mixer, so I could accept both inputs, adjust volume of each and mix them together for the speaker output. There are various small mixers available online but the cheapest were still around $50, which is more than I had spent for the entire project so far! Then I remembered my old 4-track recorder in the garage, what we used in the old days before computers and mixing software became cheap enough for the masses. I have even seen a few at thriftstores once in awhile, so you might get lucky. The 4-track unit is a bit large, but it fits in back along with the speakers just fine. The output cables from the iPod and keyboard feed into the 4-track as the mixer, adjusting the relative volumes of the inputs, then the 4-track mixed output is what connects to the new central unit for the speakers!

With the audio settled  to my satisfaction, it was time to work on the decoration again. Sadly the pipe organ didn't get as much attention its second year in the "graveyard chapel" shed, so I was already planning on a new location that would showcase decorative embellishments better. During one of my many thriftstore shopping sessions, I found a supremely tacky plastic display shelf all in silver for $1. The pattern was quite French Baroque with swirls and crosshatching, and I could visualize the shelf in the top center of the pipe box with the design repeating around the organ.

I always save foam packing sheets since I can always find a project for them, and instead of using thick gravestone foam, I had a couple sheets of thinner packing foam that wouldn't add too much bulk to the sides of the organ, while still covering the metal brackets from the side views. I decided on matching side pieces to cover the brackets with top corner pieces for the pipe box. Once I had the design sketched onto the foam, I cut the outer shapes with an electric knife, then traced the mirror images to match and cut them out too. The interior carving was done with my woodburning tool, then I painted a basecoat of black on the shelf and the foam, getting paint into all the carved grooves so no white foam was showing. After the black paint dried completely, I added gold paint accents to the design, matching the shelf and the foam pieces. Once everything was dry, I glued the foam pieces to the pipe organ, and hung the shelf from screws in the top of the pipe box. In its new Halloween home in the outer patio castle room with tapestry curtains as a backdrop, it has now reached my original vision of my Haunted Pipe Organ!

More Halloween Recipes

$\mathbf{M}$y Halloween Recipes first went online in 1997, and over the years became popular enough among fellow Halloween fans that my page reached the top of Google search results for several years in a row. Here are some new recipes including Creepy Cuisine Contest Winners. Feel free to add your own creative touches when you feel inspired!

Easier Eerie Eyeballs

I made my original Eerie Eyeball recipe the same way for years, and since I would multi-task stirring the eyeball goop melting the marshmallows and cream cheese while doing other party prep tasks, I never realized how long it really took until I filmed it. I was horrified and vowed that I would simplify the recipe! Here is an easier recipe that does not need a double-boiler or hand mixer and melts much more quickly, but also includes an easier painting technique.

2 packets plain gelatin in 1 cup tepid water
8 oz (one brick) cream cheese (can be Neufchatel)
1 10oz jar marshmallow creme (or 1 cup mini marshmallows)
1 cup cold pineapple juice

truffle candy molds or similar half-sphere molds
food coloring for irises (your choice of color)
black food coloring for pupils
piping tip or similar size lid for iris outline
solid small dowel, pen, or similar size flat round end for pupil
fine soft watercolor brush

Bloom gelatin first in tepid water. Put cream cheese into saucepan over medium heat and stir until smooth. Add marshmallows and stir until completely melted. Using marshmallow creme instead of mini marshmallows makes it melt even easier. After cream cheese and marshmallow mixture is smooth, stir in the bloomed gelatin until completely combined. Add the cold pineapple juice last, mixing again until smooth. The goop will be very runny, but after chilling it will set up into eyeball texture without being too chewy. Pour into molds and chill in fridge until set. You may still use the original melonballer technique to  scoop eyeballs from a deep container after setting, but molds are much EASIER. This full recipe makes 9 dozen truffle-mold eyeballs, however this new recipe can be easily divided in half!

After eyeballs are set, gently unmold and arrange on the serving tray. Set out food coloring on a plate or tray. Use the watercolor brush to spread a good layer of iris color large enough for the back opening of the piping tip. Dip the back opening of the piping tip into the food coloring and twist. Aim center above one eyeball, gently lower onto the eyeball surface, and gently twist to apply consistent color in a full circle. Use the watercolor brush to gently brush lines from the circle inwards, leaving white space towards the center. Dip the back of the pen into black food coloring, making sure none will drip. Gently lower the pen into the center of the painted eyeball, twisting gently to transfer all the black in a clean circle for the pupil. If the eyeball surface isn't smooth, gaps may appear in the pupil, then you can touch up with the brush if you like. Refrigerate until you are ready to serve to your eyeball eaters.

Bubbling Witches' Brew

I have made several witches' brews throughout my Halloween history, but this one is my new favorite because of the snot-like brownish-green color and the huge foamy scum bubbles filled with fog that pop open with smoke escaping from the surface. From its disgusting appearance you'd never know it's just delicious lime sherbet, pineapple juice and ginger ale!

green lime sherbet
2 quarts pineapple juice
2 liters ginger ale

Place a few scoops of lime sherbet into the cauldron or punch bowl. Pour in the pineapple juice and

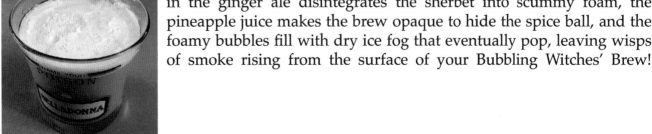

ginger ale in equal parts until the container is full. For safe dry ice, fill a large spice ball with small chunks of dry ice and place into the brew. The carbonation in the ginger ale disintegrates the sherbet into scummy foam, the pineapple juice makes the brew opaque to hide the spice ball, and the foamy bubbles fill with dry ice fog that eventually pop, leaving wisps of smoke rising from the surface of your Bubbling Witches' Brew!

Electrified Ectoplasm

This is one of my suggested experiments in the Library Laboratory. I made a special version for myself in my skull goblet, using a small tea infuser ball with a small chunk of dry ice inside, and I was extremely careful not to touch skin to the tea ball or the dry ice! The serving jar of Ectoplasm is lighted from below using the Luminescent Laboratory Libations technique, and green lime gelatin dessert glows very nicely!

Ectoplasm = green lime gelatin dessert, made according to instructions and scooped in chunks into a serving jar

Citric Acid = pineapple juice in a laboratory bottle

Tincture of Zinc = green melon liqueur in a laboratory bottle

Aqua Fortis = vodka in a laboratory bottle

"To Electrify Ectoplasm: Scoop ectoplasm into a beaker. Add citric acid, aqua fortis, and tincture of zinc. Stir gently so as not to disturb the ectoplasmic structure and release the spirits too soon. Different proportions will give you varying levels of spirits released."

Magical Mandrakes

Real mandrake roots look suspiciously like deformed babies, and have been used throughout the centuries in magical or herbal preparations. These mandrake seedlings are completely safe to eat, no ear protection required!

1 lb jar (2 cups) all natural "old-fashioned" peanut butter
1 cup powdered sugar
1 cup graham cracker crumbs
fresh celery stalk tops with leaves intact, soaked in cold water
for a few hours
chocolate candy rocks (optional)
chocolate cookie crumbs for "dirt"
drinking straws cut in half
small shot glasses or large glass container for serving

Drain the oil from the top of the jar of peanut butter. Mix drained peanut butter with powdered sugar and graham cracker crumbs with a spoon well to form peanut butter clay. Mixture will be crumbly until you knead it with your hands. Refrigerate until ready to shape. Bring to room temperature and knead again. Once smooth in texture, mold into desired shape of a crying baby. Insert a drinking straw carefully into the top of the head down into the body, and leave the straw in place while the clay is chilling so the stem hole doesn't collapse. Repeat until all mandrakes are prepared. Can store chilled for several days before serving.

When ready to serve, remove the straw, pat dry a celery leaf stalk, then insert the celery into the hole using fresh peanut butter as glue, with the leaves coming out the top. Put small candy rocks in the bottom of a small clear plastic glass, add chocolate cookie crumb "dirt" halfway, tilting the glass so the dirt is along the side, insert the baby mandrake, then fill with more dirt crumbs.

I like to provide some healthy options in my Spooky Spreads of food, but how to give fruit and vegetables some spooky style? With menacing faces of course!

Ferocious Fruit

Bosc pears
red apples
baby kiwi
your favorite fruits

For carving faces, it is best to have contrasting skin compared to the inner fruit, like Bosc pears for their nice brown skin, or red apples. As long as you have one or two faces growling in the center, you can arrange the rest of your favorite fruit any way you like. If you are very lucky, you might find baby kiwi, since when cut in half across, they look like eyeballs! Remember that many fruits will turn brown when exposed to open air, so wait to carve until right before serving, or brush exposed areas with lemon juice to keep them from turning brown.

Vicious Veggies

red or orange peppers
jicama
celery
pearl onions
carrots
broccoli
your favorite vegetables
whole cloves
toothpicks

Vegetables are a little more flexible than fruit since their cut surfaces last longer exposed to air, but they still won't last more than 24 hours without starting to change shape and wither. Jicamas are great because they have natural knobby faces you can enhance with your carving. Get inspired by the shapes you see, For instance, the curved corners of a red pepper can become devil horns. Cut pearl onions in half for googly eyes and poke a whole clove in the center for the pupil. Trim layers of white onions into teeth to add as a mouth. Break off toothpicks into smaller lengths to anchor pieces together. Celery tops can become beastly antlers, and spiky teeth are always scary!

Gingerbread Gargoyles

It's amazing what you can find on the Internet these days! While browsing cookie cutters, I happened across this giant gargoyle copper cookie cutter, so I splurged. You can also make your own cookie cutters from online kits, or you can be adventurous at the hardware store finding your own supplies. Avoid galvanized metals, but clean copper is food safe as long as you wash it well. This recipe is just as tasty with vegan substitutions. I have other sugar cookies on my menu, so I thought some Gingerbread Gargoyles would be good variety without requiring too much final decoration.

Yields about 15 1/8th-inch thick large gargoyles

1/2 cup butter (or non-dairy baking margarine)
1/2 cup molasses
1/2 cup brown sugar
1 Tbsp ginger
1 Tbsp cinnamon
1 scant tsp allspice
1 scant tsp cloves
2 tsp baking soda
1 egg (or vegan egg replacer)
2.5 cups flour

Soften the butter in the bowl. In a separate bowl, stir the spices into the brown sugar, then add to the butter and mix until creamy. Add the egg, molasses and baking soda and mix thoroughly. Add flour, then chill until set. Roll thick enough for intricate shapes like gargoyles to stay intact, at least 1/8th inch or thicker. Transfer sheet of dough to baking sheet before cutting to avoid distorting final cookie shape. Bake at 350 degrees F for about 5 minutes or until barely firm but not browned. Baking time will be longer for thicker cookies. Decorate with colored royal icing after cookies are completely cooled. Now your castle keep will be protected by Gingerbread Gargoyles, at least until they are gobbled up by guests!

Violent Vertebrae

I was lucky enough to inherit the spine used in my great-grandparents' chiropractic practice, which is a fantastic prop for this recipe! As long as you arrange the rollups in the classic spinal curvature shape with the cheese discs between, you still have a lovely display of Violent Vertebrae!

lavash bread or flour tortillas
your favorite cream cheese spread, like artichoke & spinach, etc
Colby cheese slices
round cutter same diameter as rollups
leaf lettuce (optional garnish)

Spread a thin layer of the cream cheese mixture onto lavash bread or a flour tortilla. Lavash bread is rectangular so there is less wasted after cutting into slices. Roll carefully so the cheese isn't squeezed out but tightly enough that the cheese glues the bread into a roll. Find a round cutter

that is the same diameter as your finished roll. Roll foil tightly around and chill until set enough to slice. You can quick-chill in the freezer, but frozen solid is too hard to slice. Repeat for additional rolls, since more is better as these are scarfed quickly during the party.

While the rolls are chilling, use the round cutter to cut discs from the Colby cheese. If you can't find Colby cheese or would like to use something different, find a cheese with enough color to show up against the white rollups. Save the cheese discs in plastic bags in the fridge so they do not dry out.

After the rolls are chilled enough, slice into large spine-sized rolls at least as long as they are wide. Arrange on the serving tray in a curve with a cheese disc between each roll as the spinal discs between the vertebrae. A large silver oval serving tray lined with leaf lettuce is the perfect amount of elegance for contrast when serving a spine. Voila, Violent Verterbrae!

Donut Be Scared Peekaboo Pumpkins

I have been working on recipes for see-through jack o'lantern shapes with pumpkin flavors for several years now. I recently acquired the family deep fryer, so I was finally successful with this recipe for 3 dozen mini donuts. I used a flying bat cutter upside-down as a spiky grin. I made this recipe vegan by using some simple substitutions that I have included, and they are just as delicious as the original recipe. I prefer them with a brighter orange icing or a little sparkle, but they can be served plain as well. These pumpkin donuts are easy, adorable and tasty, so Donut Be Scared!

3 ½ cups all-purpose flour
4 tsp baking powder
1 tsp salt
2 tsp ground cinnamon
1 tsp ground ginger
½ tsp baking soda
½ tsp ground nutmeg
¼ tsp ground cloves
1 cup sugar
3 Tbsp unsalted butter, room temperature (or non-dairy baking margarine)
1 large egg plus 2 egg yolks (or 2 "eggs" of vegan egg replacer)
1 tsp vanilla extract
½ cup + 1 Tbsp buttermilk (or water)
1 cup canned pure pumpkin (or 1.5 cups fresh pumpkin puree)
canola oil (for deep-frying)

Whisk first 8 dry ingredients in medium bowl to blend. Using electric mixer, beat sugar and room-temperature butter in large bowl until blended (mixture will be grainy). Beat in egg, then extra yolks and vanilla. If using fresh pumpkin puree that has more moisture than canned pumpkin, do not add buttermilk or water. Gradually beat in buttermilk if needed. Beat in one fourth of pumpkin at a time. Using rubber spatula, fold in dry ingredients in 4 additions, blending gently after each addition. Cover with plastic; chill at least 3 hours.

Sprinkle 2 rimmed baking sheets lightly with flour, even if you are using a silicone mat. Press out 1/3 of dough on floured surface to 1/2- to 2/3-inch thickness. Cut donut shapes either using 2 1/2-inch-diameter round cutter or pumpkin cutters and arrange on flour-dusted sheets. For jack o'lanterns, cut the outer pumpkin shape, arrange on sheets, then cut out the eyes & mouth after on the sheet. Drinking straws or mini triangle cutters work well for eyes, and an upside-down flying bat works well for a mouth. Repeat with remaining dough in 2 more batches. Chill dough scraps with remaining dough before rolling again. Prep one dozen from 1/3 of dough, put scraps in to chill while frying this dozen, then roll the next dozen.

Line 2 baking sheets with several layers of paper towels. Fill and heat deep fryer, or pour oil into large deep skillet to depth of 1 1/2 inches. Attach deep-fry thermometer and heat oil to 365°F to 370°F. Gently lower the jack o'lantern shape into the oil so the face does not distort. As soon as shape is set, flip over or one side will crack while frying. Fry donuts, 3 or 4 at a time, until golden brown, adjusting heat to maintain temperature, about 1 minute per side. Using slotted spoon or tongs, transfer to paper towels to drain. Cool completely before decorating. Can be frozen undecorated for 1-2 weeks and reheated in a low-temperature oven the morning of the party. See, I told you, Donut Be Scared!

Orange Pumpkin Icing

1 ½ cups powdered sugar
2 Tbsp pumpkin juice (or water)
yellow & red food coloring
orange sugar (optional)

When I roast my fresh pumpkin and strain it into puree, I save the pumpkin juice leftover from straining. You can use that for this icing for an extra boost of pumpkin goodness or use plain water. Mix the liquid and powdered sugar until smooth. Add yellow and red food coloring until you have a nice bright pumpkin orange color. Icing should be thin enough to find its own level when spreading onto donuts but not drip into the holes or off the sides. Add orange sugar while icing is still wet for extra sparkle.

Creepy Cuisine Contest Winners

I love thinking up new fun food of my own, but I also have fabulous friends who enjoy expressing their creativity. Since my parties have become so large it is difficult to prepare enough party food on my own, so I now have the Creepy Cuisine Contest each year. We have the benefit of potluck quantities of food, and my guests have a chance at the prestige of winning a prize for their creative efforts. Here are some of my favorite Creepy Cuisine Contest Winners. Thanks to everyone who granted permission to include their recipes!

Deviled Eyes
by Dave & Wendy Taubler

I love deviled eggs, and there are many ways to make them spooky. Dave & Wendy dyed the yolks and hand-painted veins on the whites with olive garnish to make these bloody Deviled Eyes. Wendy says the basic recipe is just as tasty without the bloodshot effect for other events, and is easily doubled for a larger crowd.

6 hard-boiled eggs (separated into whites and yolks)
1/3 cup creme fraiche
1/4 crumbled, cooked bacon (optional)
1 teaspoon sriracha or other spicy asian chili sauce
1 tablespoon chopped cilantro
1/2 teaspoon spicy mustard
1/4 lime zest
1 teaspoon lime juice
salt to taste
red food coloring (to your color preference)
sliced black olives

Hardboil the eggs, slice lengthwise, and put all the yolks into a mixing bowl. Mash all ingredients except olives together with the cooked yolks and add food coloring until the yolks are the desired color. Spoon yolk mixture back into egg whites. Top each half with a sliced olive as the pupil. Dip a toothpick into the red food coloring and lightly draw "bloodshot" veins across the whites. Arrange on a tray and serve to horrified guests.

Monster Toes

by Tracey Newport-Sholly

Tracey was inspired by an online recipe for mini pigs-in-blankets to make these Monster Toes. The olive toenails are the perfect touch with the green dough toes!

.

biscuit dough (purchased or your favorite homemade dough)
green food coloring
melted butter
mini smoked sausages or cocktail franks
whole black olives, pitted
toothpicks
honey mustard or ketchup (optional)

If you make your own biscuit dough, add 5 drops of green food coloring to your batter before you knead it into a light green dough. If you buy ready-made dough, tint the melted butter with green food coloring and brush the dough toes before baking.

Roll out your dough. Spread mustard or ketchup on the dough or you can reserve as dipping sauces. Cut dough into pieces large enough to cover one sausage, likely four per biscuit if using ready-made dough. Wrap the sausage in the dough, seal shut and place seam side down on a baking sheet. Cut a black olive in half. Push one half into the dough on the edge of the sausage. Use a toothpick to hold it in place as the toenail. Bake at 350 degrees for twenty minutes until they are golden green and ready for gnawing.

Frosted Bat Wings aka Demented Owls
Chocolate-Covered Bacon
by Ruth Winter

Ruth won the prize for "Most Daring Culinary Risk" with her chocolate-covered bacon. The Frosted Bat Wings were white chocolate for the frosted effect, but normal chocolate works too. Not everyone enjoys salty meat with their chocolate, but I think this recipe is mighty tasty!

Sliced raw bacon
White chocolate candy melts or milk chocolate
Decorating sugar flakes (optional)

Fry up some bacon nice & crispy. Cool it for about 15 minutes and pat off excess grease. Chop the cooked bacon into 1-inch bits. Melt the chocolate per the package instructions, microwave is easiest not to burn. Dip the cooled bits of bacon into the chocolate to cover them. Put the chocolate covered bits of bacon on wax paper. Sprinkle some sugar flakes for sparkle, then put them into the fridge to completely cool and harden the chocolate. Serve to anyone brave enough to try!

Skones with Blood Raspberry Jam

by Tracia Barbieri

Tracia found an oven-safe silicone skull pan on sale, so she cleverly thought of baking skull-shaped Skones! If you have your own favorite scone or biscuit recipe, it should work as long the dough is soft enough to take the shape of the pan while baking. Raspberry jam is a tasty way to add some bloody gore factor to an upper-crust British favorite.

2 cups all-purpose flour
1/3 cup sugar
1 tsp baking powder
¼ tsp baking soda
½ tsp salt
8 Tbsp (½ cup) unsalted butter, frozen
½ cup sour cream or plain yogurt (can be fat-free)
1 large egg
oven-safe skull pan – silicone is easiest to remove the Skones after baking

Preheat oven to 400 degrees F. Mix dry ingredients in a medium bowl. Using the large holes on a box grater, grate butter into flour mixture. Use fingers to work butter into mixture until resembles coarse meal. Whisk sour cream and egg together in separate bowl until smooth, then add to flour mixture, stirring with fork until large dough clumps form. Use your hands to press the dough against the bowl into a ball. It may be sticky but the dough will eventually come together.

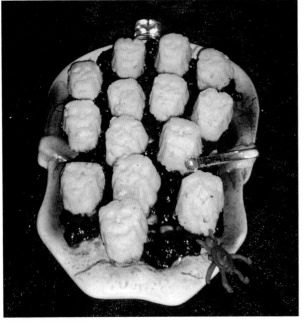

Spray the skull pan with non-stick cooking spray, even if using a silicone pan. Press dough into pan well so the dough will capture all the mold detail. Leave room for the dough to rise about a third higher. Bake until golden, about 15 minutes depending on the size of each mold. After baking, let cool in pans until shape is fully set, then unmold the Skones. Serve warm or at room temperature, over a bloodbath of raspberry jam.

Decapitare Pumpkinus Experimenti Exhibits A-J

by Lyle Seplowitz

Lyle was "experimenting" with miniature pumpkins, hence his name for this Creepy Cuisine Contest Winner. All the "decapitated" faces he drew have different personalities, and the yogurt parfait inside was absolutely delicious!

2 cups plain non-fat (or low-fat) Greek yogurt
2 tbsp or 1 oz pureed pumpkin (canned or fresh)
4 tbsp or 2 oz 100% pomegranate juice
1/4 tsp pumpkin pie spice
small bowls, or hollowed out miniature pumpkins

Hollow out miniature pumpkins out to use as bowls and draw faces on them in advance. Pour all the ingredients into a blender and mix until thoroughly combined. Taste for sweetness. Add agave nectar or honey if needed. Do not add more juice as this will make your yogurt too runny. Spoon the yogurt mixture into each pumpkin bowl. Top with either pumpkin seed granola or sliced fruit. Or both!

The Last Temptation

by Lyle Seplowitz

Lyle & Galt have brought many clever Creepy Cuisine entries over the years, and two have made it into my favorites! For The Last Temptation you can use your own favorite decadent bite-sized dessert recipe, but these clever descriptions made the presentation unique!

The Last Temptation a la mode
Remove candy corn for The Original Sin
Abstinence is for priests
Abstemiousness gets you nothing
Eat one - don't be a FUSSBUDGET
PIETY is for PRIGS

10 oz bittersweet chocolate, finely chopped
1 cup whipping cream
1 ½ Tbsp Grand Marnier or other orange liqueur
¼ cup orange marmalade
¼ cup unsweetened cocoa powder (not Dutch-processed)
64 candy corns (about 3 oz)

Line an 8x8-inch baking pan with a 12x17-inch sheet of foil or waxed paper. In a large heatproof bowl set over a saucepan of hot water, use a heatproof spatula or wooden spoon to stir together chocolate, cream, liqueur and marmalade until chocolate is melted. Scrape chocolate mixture into prepared pan, smoothing top. Chill until firm, at least 2 ½ hours or up to 1 week covered with plastic wrap.

Put cocoa powder in a shallow bowl. Lift solid chocolate mixture from pan using edges of lining foil or paper. With a long sharp knife, cut chocolate mixture into 64 squares, each about ¾-inch wide. Roll squares in cocoa powder to coat, and place one square in each paper cup. Gently press a candy corn into the top of each truffle. Store between sheets of waxed paper in an airtight container in the fridge for up to 2 weeks. Be clever writing your own sinful descriptions to provide The Last Temptation to your guests!

Glowing or Glaring Jack O Lantern Cheese Ball

by Glen Simon

Glen arrived one year with his family's traditional delicious cheese spread formed into the cutest Glaring Jack O'Lantern Cheese Ball, so I dared him to make it glow next time. He succeeded and won the next year's Creepy Cuisine Contest hands down! Use the same basic cheese mixture for either the simpler and cute glaring one, or the impressively glowing face.

16 oz (2 bricks) cream cheese
8 oz spreadable cheddar cheese (Kaukauna or similar)
2-3 oz crumbled blue cheese
1-2 tsp worcestershire sauce (to taste)
1 tbsp onion flakes
yellow & red food coloring
plastic wrap
small round bowl
pepper stem or broccoli stem

Bring all the cheeses to room temperature. Use an electric mixer to combine all ingredients into a smooth pale orange mixture. Add a few drops of yellow & red food coloring and keep mixing until you have a nice pumpkin skin color. Choose your method to continue, either the simple solid pumpkin shape or the more advanced Glowing technique.

Glaring Jack O'Lantern Cheese Ball

Also need:
pretzel pieces or other edible items to create a face

Spoon the cheese mixture into the center of a sheet of plastic wrap, pull the corners up and around to form a ball that can rest in the small round bowl. Twist all the extra plastic wrap together in a rope as tightly as possible, creating wrinkles for the grooved pumpkin skin texture. Once the rope is tight, let it twist into a knot, and press gently down into the top of the pumpkin, making the indentation for the stem. Chill at least 4-6 hours in the fridge for the cheese to set. Carefully remove the plastic wrap from the ball and set in place on the serving tray. The plastic wrap will stick a little to the cheese, making pock marks on the surface, but the grooves should stay intact. Use an offset spreader or butter knife to smooth the pocks on the surface but leave the grooves. Add either a pepper stem or a broccoli stem to be the pumpkin stem, and cut up a pretzel or using other edible items to create the adorable Glaring Jack O'Lantern Cheese Ball face.

Glowing Jack O'Lantern Cheese Ball

Also need:
round jar, juice glass or stemless wine glass
battery tealight
hard cheese in ½-inch thick slices (manchego,
parmesan, etc)
strong skewer

Select a small rounded jar, juice glass or stemless wine glass that can fit over the battery tealight and is large enough to hide inside your cheese ball. Cut the thick slices of hard cheese into the eyes & mouth shapes. Hold the jar from the inside while spreading the cheese around the back of the jar to the sides of the face area. Spread a thin layer of cheese mixture in the face area, press in the hard cheese eyes & mouth all the way to the jar surface, and spread enough mixture around to hold them in place. Keep spreading the cheese around the jar and between the facial features until you have a good thick layer around the jar in as round a shape as possible. You can use the plastic wrap technique from the Glaring version above to create wrinkles, taking care not to disturb the facial features, or smooth the final surface and leave exposed to chill, which will result in a firmer surface. Even after covering the jar with a thick layer, you will have at least half of the cheese mixture left, so you can serve a pile of cheese on the same tray, or make smaller solid pumpkins using the Glaring technique.

After completely chilled at least 4-6 hours, hold the jar from the bottom opening again while using a strong skewer to pry out the cheese eyes & mouth without disturbing the cheese mixture around them. Smooth the facial openings, then set in place on the serving tray over the battery tealight. Remember to turn on the light first! Smooth the surface with an offset spreader or butter knife, then add either a pepper stem or a broccoli stem as the pumpkin stem, and appreciate the oohs and ahhs for the Glowing Jack O'Lantern Cheese Ball!

Parting Words

Ihope you enjoyed this helping of Halloween how-tos and will be inspired to adapt these ideas to host your own haunted happenings. If you ever find yourself so deep in party plans that stress starts overtaking the joy of creativity, stop, sit back, take a deep breath, and remember this: No matter how basic or elaborate you decide to be, above all the whole point is to have fun!

Happy Haunting!

Enhanced
Eerie Elegance Extras

Spooky Shopping

Original Artwork Antique Laboratory Labels, Dastardly Dangles and other eerie items are for sale at the Britta Blvd shop on Etsy:

http://www.etsy.com/shop/brittadotcom

Truffle candy molds perfect for Easier Eerie Eyeballs:

http://www.amazon.com/Wilton-Truffles-Candy-Mold/dp/B0000CFO6Y

You can cut your own gargoyle cookies using the template on the next page, or purchase the same cookie cutter here:

http://www.amazon.com/Old-River-Road-Gargoyle-Cookie/dp/B00295QECC

If you'd like a spine model to go with your Violent Vertebrae:

http://www.amazon.com/Flexible-Desk-size-Vertebral-Column-Item/dp/B0009VLRJI
http://www.amazon.com/Lippincott-Williams-Wilkins-Chrome-Stand-SM91/dp/B000F10R66

Oven-safe silicone skull pans for Skones:

http://www.amazon.com/Wilton-Scary-Skulls-Cavity-Silicone/dp/B0036Z9WTQ
http://www.candylandcrafts.com/halloweensiliconcookiepans.htm

Pumpkin Cookie Cutter Set with Cutouts used for the Glowing Jack O' Lantern Cheese Ball:

http://www.amazon.com/OLantern-Cookie-Cutter-Assorted-Colors/dp/B001RUO7O2

Petrifying Pipe Organ Playlist

No Halloween playlist would be complete without the infamous Toccata & Fugue in D minor! You should be able to find any of these for purchase online or in music stores. I love listening to impressive joyous pipe organ music too, but I have chosen these specifically for their haunting moods for Halloween.

Toccata & Fugue in D minor BWV 565 by J.S. Bach
Passacaglia & Fugue in C minor BWV 582 by J.S. Bach
Fugue in G minor BWV 578 by J.S. Bach
Fantasy & Fugue in G minor BWV 542 by J.S. Bach
Schubler Chorales #2 BWV 646, #3 BWV 647, #4 BWV 648 by J.S. Bach
Prelude & Fugue for Organ in A minor BWV 543 by J.S. Bach
Prelude & Fugue for Organ in C minor BWV 546 by J.S. Bach
Toccata by Leo Ernest Boellman
Sonata in F minor, Op. 65: I. Allegro Moderato e Serioso by Felix Mendelssohn

Gingerbread Gargoyle Cookie Cutter Template

Trace this design onto thin cardboard & cut out,
place template on rolled cookie dough,
cut around template with a knife,
then pull away extra dough.

Ogle the Owls

Describe the location of each of the
hidden owls.

1. ....

2. ....

3. ....

4. ....

5. ....

6. ....

7. ....

8. ....

9. ....

10. ....

11. ....

12. ....

13. ....

14. ....

15. ....

16. ....

17. ....

18. ....

19. ....

20. ....

21. ....

Name _____

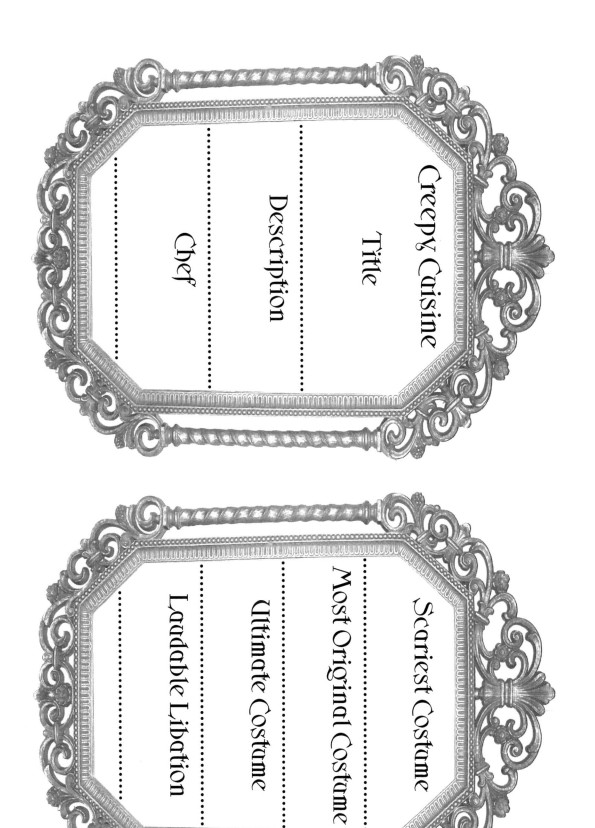

Creepy Cuisine

Title

....

Description

....

Chef

....

Scariest Costume

....

Most Original Costume

....

Ultimate Costume

....

Laudable Libation

....

About the Author

Britta Peterson

Enhanced Eerie Elegance is Britta's second book after 15 years of self-publishing her website Britta Blvd, where she is known as the "Webmistress of the Dark." Artistic and crafty from a young age, over the years she has turned holidays into opportunities for elaborate parties as performance art, transforming her home into an entirely new environment, especially for Halloween. Friends have called her "a cross between Martha Stewart and Tim Burton," which is a comparison she considers high praise. She currently lives in Santa Clara, California, with her two black cats with pumpkin-orange eyes, Ebony and Onyx, who are too much of a handful to be in the same portrait, but you can spy Ebony supervising the Ghostly Greenery.

Made in the USA
Lexington, KY
02 September 2013